NATURE DETECTIVE

British Wild Flowers

Victoria Munson

WAYLAND

First published in 2015 by Wayland
Copyright © Wayland 2015

Wayland
338 Euston Road
London NW1 3BH

Wayland Australia
Level 17/207 Kent Street
Sydney, NSW 2000

Designer: Elaine Wilkinson
Consultant: Michael Scott, OBE

A cataloguing record for this title is available
at the British Library.
Dewey number: 582.1'3'0941-dc23
ISBN: 978 0 7502 9276 4
ebook: 978 0 7502 9326 6

Printed in China

Wayland, part of Hachette Children's Group and
published by Hodder and Stoughton Limited.
www.hachette.co.uk

Picture acknowledgements:
iStock: 13 AntiMartina; 36 Savushkin; 40
Bluefly06; Shutterstock: 4t stocker1970; 5b
BlueRingMedia; 6t MarkMirror; 6b Roger Hall; 7
wawritto; 8t Fedorov Oleksiy; 8c Jag_cz; 8b Kletr;
8r photka; 9t Dionisvera; 9r Valentina Razumova;
9b NinaM; 10 Lostry7; 11 Tom Curtis; 12 Dani
Vincek; 14 PozitivStudija; 15 FotograFFF; 16
Sternstunden; 17 Lee Prince; 18 Ruud Morijn
Photographer; 19 Gala_Kan; 20 Bildagentur
Zoonar GmbH; 21 Christian Musat; 22 wjarek; 23
chris2766; 24 BeppeNob; 25 Alexandru Teodor
Chirila; 26 Inger Anne Hulbækdal; 27 karloss;
28 Gala_Kan; 29 Vasilius; 30 Simon Greig; 31
Colette3; 32 Ivonne Wierink; 33 Olga Kovalenko;
34 BestPhotoStudio; 35 Ivan Tihelka; 37t Tim
UR; 37b Steve McWilliam; 38 Mark Mirror;
39 Bildagentur Zoonar GmbH; 41 Aleksandr
Stepanov; 42 Mark Herreid; 43 Martin Fowler; 44
hadot 760; 45 Shutterschock; 46 Andrew Roland;
47 Imladris; 48 MarkMirror; 49 LensTravel; 50
Kefca; 51 Bildagentur Zoonar GmbH; 52 Martin
Fowler; 53 Tompet; 54 Diana Taliun; 55 Vahan
Abrahamyan; 56 hanmon; 57 Janis Smits; 58t
Maria Uspenskaya; 58c kritskaya; 58b DeepGreen;
59 Peter Bull

With thanks to Lily and Polly

Contents

Be a nature detective!

To be a nature detective, you need to be observant. This means looking carefully around you. Flowers can be found in all kinds of places such as in woods, fields and hedges, near water or even between cracks in the pavement.

A bluebell wood

Getting out and about

Different flowers grow well in different habitats. You can find wild flowers in your garden, school and local area. Or you can find them on a walk through woodland, along a river or by the sea. You could ask to visit somewhere new at a weekend, or for a school trip. If you're going out for a nature walk, you may need to wear wellies and a waterproof jacket. Take a notebook and pens. Once you have taken down some notes, try to do a drawing. This will help you with identification later, if you don't have this guidebook with you.

Colour pencils

Wellies

Notebook

Waterproof jacket

Heather

Identifying flowers

Flowers are all shapes, colours and sizes. By knowing the parts of a flower, you can make better notes to help you identify them. There are various features you can write down, such as their size, shape, colour and where you saw them.

Parts of a flower

A flower has several parts. The stem, also called the stalk, holds the flower up. The outer part of the flower is a ring of sepals. These are small and green, and protect the flower when it is in bud. Inside these are the petals, which are brightly coloured to attract insects.

Inside the flower is the carpel, the female part of the flower. It looks like a long-necked vase. The top of the carpel is called the stigma. The stigma's job is to catch the pollen. The long neck part is called the style and it holds up the stigma. The bottom, fatter part is the ovary containing the ovules, or eggs.

The male parts of the flower are called the stamens. The stamens have two parts – the anther, which produces the pollen, and the filament that holds up the anther. Pollen is carried from the stigma of one flower to another.

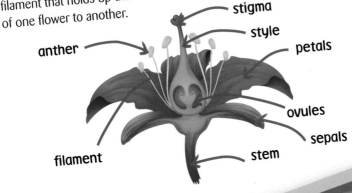

anther • stigma • style • petals • ovules • sepals • filament • stem

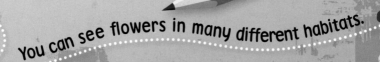

You can see flowers in many different habitats.

Flower life cycle

When a seed is planted, roots start to grow down into the soil to hold it in place. The shoots grow up through the soil towards the light. Above ground, the shoots get bigger and bigger and grow leaves. Some plants have one tall stem; others have one stem with lots of branches coming from it. At the ends of the branches, flowers appear.

Pollination

Pollination is the process that allows flowers to produce their seeds. Some flowers can pollinate themselves. In others, pollen is carried between flowers by the wind or by insects such as butterflies and bees. The pollen sticks onto the insect's body and is rubbed off in the next flower. When pollen lands on the stigma, it produces a tube that grows down the style into the ovary. It joins with the egg cells (ovules), which then develop into the seeds. The petals can now fall off, their job done.

Butterflies and bees collect pollen from flowers.

Photosynthesis

Plants make their own food in a process called photosynthesis. This means that they use sunlight, water and a gas called carbon dioxide to make glucose, a kind of sugar. At night-time, plants take in carbon dioxide from the air and water from the soil. In the daytime, plants use energy from sunlight to turn water and carbon dioxide into glucose. Plants use this glucose to help them grow.

In a plant's leaves is a substance called chlorophyll, which makes leaves green. Chlorophyll is important because it traps energy from the sun so that the plant can use it in photosynthesis.

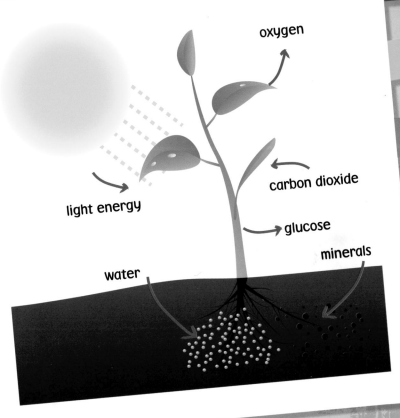

oxygen

carbon dioxide

light energy

glucose

minerals

water

Features of flowers

To help you recognise flowers, their features, such as their leaves, fruits and petals, are described in a particular way. Leaves are many different shapes and can be lobed or toothed. They can also be seen on the stem in whorls (rings), in a spiral or in pairs.

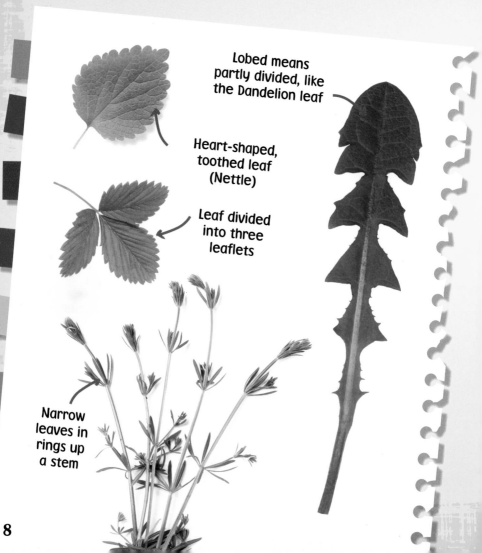

Lobed means partly divided, like the Dandelion leaf

Heart-shaped, toothed leaf (Nettle)

Leaf divided into three leaflets

Narrow leaves in rings up a stem

You can recognise a plant by looking at its fruits and seeds. Most of the seeds are inside the fruit. Some fruits can be eaten by humans, while others are only safe for birds and animals to eat. Always check whether a fruit is safe to eat.

Blackberries

Strawberries

Rosehips

Scientific names

Scientists divide plants and animals into groups to help them to categorise and identify them. Each living thing has a common name as well as a scientific name, such as Dandelion which is *Taraxacum officinale*. The common name can be different around the world, and even within the same country, whereas the scientific name is the same all over the world.

Common Mallow

Scientific name: *Malva sylvestris*
Height: 45–90 cm
Family: Mallow
Habitat: Roadsides and grassy areas
Flowers: June to October

Common Mallow has notched, pink petals that have dark purple veins on them. The strong, thick stalk is hairy. Leaves are large and dark green with five lobes. The leaves look crinkly when the plant is young. It can survive without water for a long time.

The ancient Romans used to grow Mallow for food and medicine.

Red Campion

Scientific name: *Silene dioica*
Height: up to 90 cm
Family: Pink
Habitat: Woods, hedges and cliffs
Flowers: May to October

In warm winters, Red Campion can continue flowering all year.

These bright pink flowers sit on the top of long stems. Leaves are oval with a pointed tip, sitting in pairs on the stems spread apart from each other. The five petals have a deep split in them so it looks like they actually have ten petals. White Campion look the same as Red Campion but has white flowers.

Ragged-Robin

Latin name: *Lychnis flos-cuculi*
Height: up to 75 cm
Family: Pink
Habitat: Damp meadows and marshes
Flowers: May to July

These deep-pink
flowers have five petals
divided into four narrow lobes
and they always look quite tatty, or
'ragged'. The stems have stiff hairs on them
and the leaves are pointed and thin like grass.

12

Field Bindweed

Latin name: *Convolvulus arvensis*
Height: 20–75 cm
Family: Bindweed
Habitat: Fields, gardens and waste ground
Flowers: June to September

This pretty flower is in fact a pest for farmers and gardeners because it has long roots that are hard to get rid of. The roots can stretch up to 2 metres underground. Its thin, twisty stem wraps itself tightly around other plants for support. Flowers can be pale pink, white or pink and white-striped and they smell sweet. Leaves are grey-green pointed ovals.

13

Heather

Scientific name: *Calluna vulgaris*
Height: up to 60 cm
Family: Heather
Habitat: Heathland, moors and hillsides
Flowers: July to September

Heather twigs have been used to make brooms, baskets, rope and bedding.

Heather is a small shrub that grows low to the ground. Its tough, woody stems grow upright and are covered in lots of tiny pinky-purple flowers.

Rosebay Willowherb

Scientific name: *Chamerion angustifolium*
Height: 30–120 cm
Family: Willowherb
Habitat: Woodland clearings and waste ground
Flowers: June to September

Rosebay
Willowherb
is also known as
'fire weed' as it was
one of the first plants
to appear in bombed
ground during the
World Wars.

Rosebay Willowherb is a
tall straight plant with a dense
head of pink-purple flowers. The
flowers and leaves are arranged in spirals
up the thick stem. Each flower is made up of
four petals, with the upper pair wider than the
lower pair. Leaves are long, thin and pointed. Its
pink-purple fruit is shaped like a narrow cylinder.

15

Foxglove

Scientific name: *Digitalis purpurea*
Height: 50–150 cm
Family: Figwort
Habitat: Hedges, woods and grassland
Flowers: June to September

This plant has 20–30 bell-shaped, purply-pink flowers, which grow at the top of a tall, stiff stem. Each flower has dark spots on its lower lip. The leaves are oval and wrinkled. However, although these flowers might look pretty, they are actually extremely poisonous!

 One Foxglove can have up to 80 bell-shaped flowers.

Harebell

Scientific name: *Campanula rotundifolia*
Height: 15–50 cm
Family: Bellflower
Habitat: Heaths and grassland
Flowers: July to October

Honey bees can often be found feeding on Harebells.

These delicate, bell-shaped lilac flowers are widespread and common across Britain. They grow on slender, upright stems. Long, thin leaves are found at the bottom of the plant.

Common Comfrey

Scientific name: *Symphytum officinale*
Height: 30–120 cm
Family: Borage
Habitat: Damp places near
streams, rivers and ponds
Flowers: May to July

Mushed-up leaves of Comfrey were put onto wounds and burns to soothe them.

The flowers of this plant are very distinctive as they are groups of small, drooping, tubular flowers that are usually purple, but are also found as white or pink. The stems are covered in bristly hairs. Leaves are large, hairy ovals.

Tufted Vetch

Scientific name: *Vicia cracca*
Height: 60–200 cm
Family: Pea
Habitat: Hedgerows and meadows
Flowers: June to August

This tall, climbing plant has long stems and striking violet-purple flowers. Leaves are made up of 8–12 pairs of leaflets. Between 10 and 40 tube-shaped flowers hang down mainly on one side of the stem. You can spot seed pods on the plant in summer, which turn black when ripe.

Common Teasel

Scientific name: *Dipsacus fullonum*
Height: 50–200 cm
Family: Teasel
Habitat: Woods, waste ground and roadsides
Flowers: July and August

Goldfinches love eating the Teasel's seeds.

This prickly plant has a stiff, square stem covered in hooked prickles, with thin spiky leaves and a spiky flower head. In summer, the large flower head is covered in tiny lilac flowers.

Spear Thistle

Scientific name: *Cirsium vulgare*
Height: up to 1.5 m
Family: Daisy
Habitat: Grassland and waste ground
Flowers: July to September

We can tell these plants easily by their pointed, spear-shaped leaves that stick out from the thick stem. There are also sharp spines underneath the flower head to stop animals eating them. The flower head is oval-shaped and covered in pinky-purple florets. This eventually turns into a fluffy seedball.

Common Poppy

Scientific name: *Papaver rhoeas*
Height: 20–60 cm
Family: Poppy
Habitat: Fields and hedgerows
Flowers: June to September

Common Poppies are also known as Field Poppies because of where they are found most often.

Unmistakable in fields
of crops or by a roadside,
these bright red flowers can be seen
all through the summer. The upright
stems support four broad, overlapping petals
2–4 cm wide. The petals often have a black blotch
at the base. The stem and leaves are covered with hairs.

Scarlet Pimpernel

Scientific name: *Anagallis arvensis*
Height: 5–20 cm
Family: Primrose
Habitat: Fields, gardens and sand dunes
Flowers: June to August

These orangey-red flowers sit on top of a thin branch that comes off a thick stalk. Oval leaves grow in pairs up the stalk. Each flower has five petals that are about 14 mm across. Seeds grow in a round capsule.

Scarlet Pimpernels close their petals when it rains.

Meadow Buttercup

Scientific name: *Ranunculus acris*
Height: up to 1 m
Family: Buttercup
Habitat: Damp meadows, fields and grassy places
Flowers: May to September

The Meadow Buttercup is one of the tallest types of buttercup. It is recognisable by its five bright yellow, shiny petals and its long, upright stem, surrounded by whorls of thin, pointed green leaves. They have smooth, round, unfurrowed stalks.

Creeping Buttercup

Scientific name: *Ranunculus repens*
Height: up to 60 cm
Family: Buttercup
Habitat: Damp places, waste ground and gardens
Flowers: May to October

You can tell Creeping Buttercup from Meadow Buttercup by its furrowed flower stalks. It is a troublesome weed in gardens. Its long, leafy runners spread quickly, and produce new flower stems regularly along their length. If you try to dig them up or plough them, any runner left behind grows into new plants.

Common Bird's-foot-trefoil

Scientific name: *Lotus corniculatus*
Height: 5–20 cm
Family: Pea
Habitat: Fields, heaths and coasts
Flowers: May to September

This flower is also called 'Eggs and Bacon' because of its yolk-coloured flowers and red buds like bacon.

The flowers of this common plant have bright yellow petals that are sometimes streaked with red. Its weak stems lie close to the ground. Its fruit pods are long and claw-like, which give it the name 'bird's-foot'. Its leaves have five leaflets but two of these are at the foot of the leaf stalk, so it looks like there are just three leaflets. The word 'trefoil' means 'three-leaved'.

Dandelion

Scientific name: *Taraxacum officinale*
Height: 5–40 cm
Family: Daisy
Habitat: Fields, roadsides and grassy places
Flowers: March to October

Dandelion leaves can be eaten in salads or used to make wine and tea.

Dandelions are familiar plants with their heads of bright yellow florets. In late summer, the florets develop into 'dandelion clocks'. These are clusters of small, singled-seeded fruits, each with a tuft of white hairs at the tip. The hairs spread the seeds in the wind like a parachute.

Perforate St John's-Wort

Scientific name: *Hypericum perforatum*
Height: up to 80 cm
Family: St John's Wort
Habitat: Chalky soil, open woodland and grassy areas
Flowers: June to September

St John's-Wort has been used for many centuries as a herbal remedy.

This stiffly upright plant, with branching stems, is covered in small yellow flowers. The flowers have five sepals and five yellow petals with black dots on the edge of them. Leaves are oval.

Tansy

Scientific name: *Tanacetum vulgare*
Height: up to 75 cm
Family: Daisy
Habitat: Fields and waste ground
Flowers: July to October

Common throughout Britain,
these bright yellow flowers have
strong, upright stalks. The strongly scented
flower heads are flat and about 7–12 mm across.
Each of the leaves is split into finely, toothed leaflets,
making them look a bit like fern leaves.

Wild Daffodil

Scientific name: *Narcissus pseudonarcissus*
Height: up to 50 cm
Family: Amaryllis
Habitat: Woods, fields and orchards
Flowers: March and April

The Daffodil is the national symbol of Wales.

The yellow, funnel-shaped flowers of Daffodils are a sure sign that spring has arrived. Big, showy garden varieties are widely planted in gardens, parks and on roundabouts and often escape into the wild. True wild daffodils are smaller, with paler flowers. They are only found in southern Britain.

Yellow Iris

Scientific name: *Iris pseudacorus*
Height: 40–150 cm
Family: Iris
Habitat: Streams, rivers, marshes and woods
Flowers: June to August

The striking Yellow Iris is also called 'Yellow Flag' because its drooping petals look like a flag in the wind. This species is mostly found by water and has tall, sword-shaped leaves. Each stem holds 2–3 large flowers. Each flower has three parts that curve down and three parts that curve up.

Lesser Celandine

Scientific name: *Ranunculus ficaria*
Height: 5–25 cm
Family: Buttercup
Habitat: Woods, hedgerows and grassy banks
Flowers: March to May

Very similar-looking to a Buttercup, this yellow, star-shaped flower has 7–12 petals that are spread out from each other. The dark green leaves are heart-shaped and toothed. In spring, they cover woodland floors in every direction.

The Lesser Celandine opens only when the sun shines.

Marsh Marigold

Scientific name: *Caltha palustris*
Height: 30 cm
Family: Buttercup
Habitat: Marshes, damp woodland and meadows
Flowers: March to July

The Marsh Marigold is also known as 'Kingcup'.

This member of the Buttercup family only grows in damp places. Its flowers are 20–50 mm across, with five to eight bright yellow lobes. These are greenish underneath.

Shepherd's Purse

Scientific name: *Capsella bursa-pastoris*
Height: up to 35 cm
Family: Cabbage
Habitat: Gardens and farmland
Flowers: All year round

Small birds, such as chaffinches, enjoy eating the seeds from this flower.

These tall, thin flowers are named after their heart-shaped seed pods, which look like a pouch that a shepherd might carry. They have four upright sepals that surround the four notched, white petals. Leaves are small, flat and triangular.

Cuckoo Flower

Scientific name: *Cardamine pratensis*
Height: up to 60 cm
Family: Cabbage
Habitat: Damp meadows and by water
Flowers: April to June

The Cuckoo Flower got its name because it begins to flower at a similar time to the Cuckoo bird arriving in Britain from Africa. Its tall, upright stems support the petals, which are lilac at first but gradually lighten until they are white. Leaves are rounded and toothed.

Cuckoo Flowers' petals, leaves and stalks can be eaten in a salad.

Dog-Rose

Scientific name: *Rosa canina*
Height: 1–3 m
Family: Rose
Habitat: Hedgerows and woods
Flowers: June and July

Rosehips are used to make tea, syrup and itching powder.

Dog-Roses have lightly scented white flowers measuring 6 cm across. The flowers can also be pale pink or dark pink. In the middle of the plants are many stamens with yellow anthers. The flowers turn into a rounded fruit called rosehip. Its stems, like all roses, are covered in sharp prickles. Its dark green, toothed leaves are oval with a pointed tip.

Bramble

Scientific name: *Rubus fruticosa*

Height: 2 m

Family: Rose

Habitat: Hedges, woods, coasts and gardens

Flowers: June to August

In Scotland, people use the name 'bramble' for the fruits too.

Often known as Blackberry plants, Brambles have whitish-pink flowers. Five petals surround prominent anthers which change from white to brown. The flowers produce berries which begin green, turn red and then develop into juicy blackberries. Spiky thorns help the stems scramble over surrounding plants.

Wild Strawberry

Scientific name: *Fragaria vesca*
Height: 5–30 cm tall
Family: Rose
Habitat: Woodland, hedges and scrubland
Flowers: April to July

Wild Strawberries are smaller and tastier than the cultivated fruits of gardens and farms. The white, five-petalled flowers develop into small, juicy, red fruits, with seeds on their outside skin. Strawberry leaves are heart-shaped and toothed. Long, creeping stems, called runners, produce rooted clumps of leaves which develop into new strawberry plants.

Meadowsweet

Scientific name: *Filipendula ulmaria*
Height: up to 120 cm
Family: Rose
Habitat: Damp meadows, marshes, streams and rivers
Flowers: June to September

Meadowsweet was used in Tudor times to make houses smell nice.

Meadowsweet gets its name because its flowers have a strong, sweet smell. It has a spray of tiny creamy-white flowers. The stamens are longer than the petals. Stems are tall and straight and the leaves are in 3–5 pairs of oval, pointed leaflets, dark green on top and pale downy-white underneath.

Cow Parsley

Scientific name: *Anthriscus sylvestris*
Height: 60–100 cm
Family: Carrot
Habitat: Hedgerows, fields, roadside verges
Flowers: April to June

Cow Parsley is called 'Queen Anne's Lace' after its frilly leaves.

These tall plants have clusters of white flowers on flat flower heads. Many branches of flower heads come from one tall stem, which look like the spokes of an umbrella. Its leaves are finely divided into many pairs of toothed leaflets, so they look rather fern-like. This plant is often confused with Hemlock.

Hemlock

Scientific name: *Conium maculatum*
Height: up to 2 m
Family: Carrot
Habitat: Wasteland, ditches and roadsides
Flowers: June and July

Hemlock is extremely poisonous to animals and humans. It looks similar to Cow Parsley but its clusters of flowers are more dome-shaped and its leaves look lacier. Hemlock also has purple spots on its long, hairless stems. The flowers are only 2 mm across and have five evenly spaced white, heart-shaped petals. Its crushed leaves have a disgusting smell.

Yarrow

Scientific name: *Achillea millefolium*
Height: 10–45 cm
Family: Daisy
Habitat: Meadows, gardens and hedgerows
Flowers: June to August

Yarrow has a strong, sweet scent.

Yarrow is in the Daisy Family. That means its 'flowers' are actually tight heads of tiny florets. The outer florets have broad lobes that look like five white or pinkish petals around the central florets. These flower heads are arranged in a dense, showy, flat-topped cluster. Its leaves look feathery.

White Clover

Scientific name: *Trifolium repens*
Height: up to 30 cm
Family: Pea
Habitat: Fields and grassy places
Flowers: May to October

Red Clover looks the same as White Clover but with red petals.

This very common low-growing plant is found in grassy places with Daisies, Buttercups and Dandelions. It has clusters of tiny white, or pinkish, flowers on thin, upright stalks. The leaves have three round leaflets, marked with a pale 'v' shape.

43

Common Daisy

Scientific name: *Bellis perennis*
Height: 4–12 cm
Family: Daisy
Habitat: Fields, meadows and gardens
Flowers: March to October

Daisies got their name from the words 'day's eye' because they close at night and open in the daytime.

Daisy 'flowers' are actually a head made up of hundreds of tiny florets. Each outer floret produces a single white 'ray'. These make the white rim, like petals around the head. A large number of 'disc florets' together form the yellow button in the centre.

Ox-eye Daisy

Scientific name: *Leucanthemum vulgare*
Height: 20–70 cm
Family: Daisy
Habitat: Grassy places and roadsides
Flowers: June to October

Ox-eye Daisies are much bigger than Common Daisies and are Britain's largest native Daisy, reaching up to 6 cm across. Their lobed leaves are dark green and grow in spirals up its stem. The Ox-eye Daisy is nicknamed 'Moon Daisy' because its large white flower head appears to glow in the evening light.

Garlic Mustard

Scientific name: *Alliaria petiolata*
Height: up to 1 m
Family: Cabbage
Habitat: Woods, hedgerows and
  roadside verges
Flowers: April to June

Orange-tip butterflies often lay their eggs on Garlic Mustard.

Also known as 'Jack-by-the-hedge',
this plant can often be found in large
numbers across a woodland floor. On top of
the strong stems are small white flowers about 6 mm
across with four petals. The seeds grow in long green pods
that turn brown and remain on the flower through the summer.
If you crush the heart-shaped leaves, they smell of garlic.

Ramsons

Scientific name: *Allium ursinum*
Height: 25–45 cm
Family: Lily
Habitat: Damp woodland, hedges
and by rivers and streams
Flowers: April to June

Ramsons can be found in large
groups in damp woodland. It is also
known as 'Wild Garlic' because the dark
green leaves smell of garlic when crushed.
The delicate white flowers have six thin petals
and six stamens with white anthers.

Wood Anemone

Scientific name: *Anemone nemorosa*
Height: 6–30 cm
Family: Buttercup
Habitat: Woodland
Flowers: March to May

These low-growing woodland
flowers start to open as soon as there
are some good spells of spring sunshine.
The white, star-shaped flowers sit on a thin,
red stem, above deeply lobed leaves. Petals have grey
veins and in the middle are distinctive yellow anthers.

48

Lily-of-the-Valley

Scientific name: *Convallaria majalis*
Height: up to 25 cm
Family: Lily
Habitat: Woodlands
Flowers: May and June

Lily-of-the-Valley is a sweet-scented flower that has tiny bell-shaped white flowers just 8 mm wide. Bright-green leaves are large and oval-shaped. Its fruit is a small orange berry that holds brown seeds.

Common Snowdrop

Scientific name: *Galanthus nivalis*
Height: up to 20 cm
Family: Onion
Habitat: Woodland, gardens, hedgerows and churchyards
Flowers: January to March

It used to be thought unlucky to bring Snowdrops into your house.

Snowdrops appear at the beginning of the year as soon as the weather warms up after winter. Each flower has three outer petals and three inner ones. Dark green leaves are long and thin.

Cleavers

Scientific name: *Galium aparine*
Height: up to 1.5 m
Family: Bedstraw
Habitat: Hedges, farms, waste ground
Flowers: May to September

The stems of this sticky plant have backward-pointing prickles. Bits of stem easily break off and get attached by their prickles onto animal fur, feathers and even clothes. The stem fragments then fall and grow into new plants. Cleavers has thin green leaves in whorls of 6–8 around the stem. In summer, its tiny white, star-shaped flowers develop into small, hooked fruits which are also spread in fur.

Stinging Nettle

Scientific name: *Urtica dioica*
Height: 30–150 cm
Family: Nettle
Habitat: Farmland, fields and gardens
Flowers: June to September

These common weeds are well-known to all. The dark green, heart-shaped, toothed leaves can give a nasty sting, as can the sharp hairs on the stem. However, they don't sting insects, and many butterflies, such as the Peacock and the Red Admiral, lay eggs on them. The hatched caterpillars then eat the nettle leaves.

Cooked nettles can be added to soups, stews and tea.

White Deadnettle

Scientific name: *Lamium album*
Height: 20–60 cm
Family: Mint
Habitat: Hedges, roadsides and waste ground
Flowers: May to December

White Deadnettle look very similar to a Stinging Nettle, but unlike the Stinging Nettle, it has creamy white flowers at the top of square stems. The flowers have an unusual curved hood and a lip. Heart-shaped, toothed leaves are covered in fine hair. Red Deadnettle looks the same as White Deadnettle but has purplish-pink flowers.

Field Forget-Me-Not

Scientific name: *Myosotis arvensis*
Height: 15–30 cm
Family: Borage
Habitat: Woods, hedges and gardens
Flowers: April to September

Forget-Me-Nots have been used in herbal medicine to help with eye diseases.

These small, low-growing plants love dry, sunny places. Each tiny flower has five blue petals with a yellow 'eye' in the centre. The oblong leaves are grey-green, hairy and stalkless. The thin stem is a bit hairy.

Viper's Bugloss

Scientific name: *Echium vulgare*
Height: 30–90 cm
Family: Borage
Habitat: Dry grassland, sand dunes and cliff tops
Flowers: June to September

Because its stems are spotted like a snake's skin, Viper's Bugloss was once used as a cure for snake bites.

These stiff, upright plants have prickly hairs on the thick stem. The flowers are a bright-blue trumpet-shape with long red stamens. The buds are pink. Painted Lady butterflies love this flower, but it can irritate human skin so don't touch it!

55

Bluebell

Scientific name: *Hyacinthoides non-scripta*
Height: 20–50 cm
Family: Asparagus
Habitat: Woodland
Flowers: April to June

Bluebells are in full bloom
in May, sometimes covering forest
floors with thousands of flowers. The flowers
are small, drooping purply-blue bell shapes. Flowering
in early spring means they can get most sunlight before
the trees are in full leaf. Leaves are narrow and glossy green.

The flowers are edible and taste a bit like cucumber.

Cornflower

Scientific name: *Centaurea cyanus*
Height: up to 80 cm
Family: Daisy
Habitat: Fields, meadows and roadside verges
Flowers: July and August

Cornflowers are very rare but numbers have recently started to increase because of campaigns to reintroduce them. They are now being seeded in meadows and sold in wild flower seed packs for people to sow in their gardens. On top of a long, greyish stem, they have star-shaped outer florets, with smaller, thin purply florets in the middle. Its leaves are long and thin.

How to protect wild flowers

Wild flowers are disappearing. This is because their habitats have been destroyed by new buildings and roads, and by the use of weedkillers in farming. Many weeds of the fields, such as Poppy and Cornflower, are declining in numbers.

Some farmers and local councils now allow hedges and roadside verges to grow wild to encourage plants. Many areas have now become protected, such as some nature reserves and parks. You could visit a nature reserve or woodlands to learn more about wild flowers and their habitats.

There are also many organisations dedicated to protecting flowers. See the list of websites and places to visit on pages 60–61 for more information.

You can help to protect nature by planting flowers in your garden. Why not create a wild patch in one corner of your garden by scattering some seeds and letting them grow tall? Plant different species and see what insects they attract.

You will need:
- soil
- a trowel
- packets of seeds
- a watering can
- a window box or basket

Make a wild-flower window box

You can get all of these from your local garden centre.

1 Place the soil into the box or basket. Break up the soil with the trowel or your hands to let air into the soil. Remove any large stones.

2 Make a furrowed line in the soil with your finger.

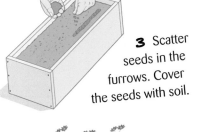

3 Scatter seeds in the furrows. Cover the seeds with soil.

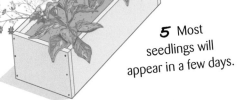

4 Water them a little bit. Don't flood the soil or the plants won't grow.

5 Most seedlings will appear in a few days.

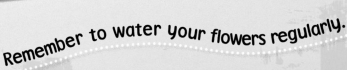

Remember to water your flowers regularly.

Further information

Places to visit

Royal Botanic Gardens at Kew
Richmond
Surrey TW9 3AB
www.rbgkew.org.uk

Royal Botanic Garden, Edinburgh
Inverleith Row
Edinburgh EH3 5LR
www.rbge.org.uk

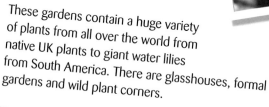

These gardens contain a huge variety of plants from all over the world from native UK plants to giant water lilies from South America. There are glasshouses, formal gardens and wild plant corners.

National Wildflower Centre
Court Hey Park
Roby Road
Knowsley
Liverpool L16 3NA
www.nwc.org.uk
The National Wildflower Centre aims to raise awareness of the importance of wildflowers to the environment. It has seasonal displays and encourages people to create their own wildflower areas.

National Trust
www.nationaltrust.org.uk/visit/places/find-a-place-to-visit/

Find a new place to visit by searching for gardens and parks or coasts and countryside in your local area or further afield.

Useful websites

www.wildlifetrusts.org.uk

The website for The Wildlife Trusts gives you a list of nature reserves that you can visit as well as a brilliant species explorer guide for animals, marine wildlife, plants and fungi.

www.plantlife.org.uk/wild_plants/plant_species/

An A-Z of wild flowers with descriptions and photographs.

www.seasonalwildflowers.com

This brilliant site lists flowers that you might see month by month as well as providing detailed information and photographs.

www.nwc.org.uk/visitor_centre/plant_id_guide

The National Wildflower Centre has a useful wild flower plant identification guide with pictures and further information.

Useful books

Plant Life: Flower Power, Living Leaf, Roots and Shoots, Seed Safari by Judith Heneghan (Wayland, 2014)

See How Plants Grow by Nicola Edwards (Wayland, 2011)

Wildlife Wonders: Why Do Plants Have Flowers? by Pat Jacobs (Watts, 2014)

How many different flowers can you spot in your local area?

Glossary

anther the part of the flower that produces pollen

berry fleshy fruit containing seeds

bloom when a flower is fully open

bud a flower before it blooms

carpel the female parts of a flower

chlorophyll a substance in plants that makes leaves green

filament the part of a plant that holds up the anther

floret small flowers

flower head a cluster of small flowers that often look like one flower

furrowed grooved or dented

fruit the part of a plant that holds the seeds

habitat a place where a plant or an animal lives in the wild

leaflet the small separate parts of a leaf

lobed rounded or sticking out

native belonging to a place or country

ovary the female part of a flower containing the ovules

ovules the 'eggs' in a flower which develop into seeds after pollination

petals the showy parts of the flower which attract insects

photosynthesis the process a plant uses to turn water and carbon dioxide into glucose using sunlight

pollen the male powder found in flowers

pollination the spread of pollen from one flower to another so it can make seeds

runners stems that runs along the ground

sepals parts of a flower that protect it when it is a bud

shrub a low-growing woody plant with many stems

stamen the male part of a flower

stigma the top part of the carpel in a flower where pollen is caught

style the part of a flower that holds up the stigma

unfurrowed smooth with no groove or dent

whorls rings of leaves around the stem of a plant

Index

Become a nature detective and discover how to identify common British wildlife with these fantastic titles:

9780750283410

9780750292764

9780750292849

9780750283427

9780750292856

9780750292085

Let's investigate!